THE DISCIPLE'S

Wedding

Planning a Wedding That
Gives Glory to
God

By
Nancy Orr
with
Kay McKean

DEDICATION

To my husband Jim who gave much encouragement as I wrote; to Kay McKean and Sheila Jones who have poured themselves out to make this book a reality; to hundreds of couples who have provided me with the experiences to be able to write this, and most of all, to God who gave me the talents, provided the training and walked me through the years of growth. To God be all of the glory, honor and praise.

The Disciple's Wedding
copyright © 1994 by Discipleship Publications International
One Merrill Street, Woburn, MA 01801

Edited by Sheila Jones

ISBN 1-884553-21-4

Contents

MINDSET

1

Introduction

KEEPING A SPIRITUAL MINDSET
BY KAY MCKEAN

"WILL YOU MARRY ME?" Those are the four sweet words every woman in love is ecstatic to hear. It's followed, usually, by a resounding, "YES!" Then there's the usual engagement ring, announcements, congratulations, and the date is set. And now begins the work of planning the best wedding ceremony of all time: yours! Those words lead to weeks or months of preparing for the commitment of yourself to another for the rest of your life.

As important as those words may be, it is imperative not to forget several other words that you have said: "What is your confession?" "JESUS IS LORD!" This vow, above all others, was the vow that you made when you became a Christian; the decision you made to follow Jesus and humbly accept his forgiveness as you were baptized into Christ. At that time, you made the commitment to give yourself to Jesus, to be a disciple for the rest of your life. And now, as disciples, you and your future husband will be joined together to serve God as a married couple.

Vows are not to be taken lightly. As we read the Bible, we can see the attitude God has toward the vows that people make to him. What we promise, God expects us to DO! In Ecclesiastes 5:4 we read: "When you make a vow to God, do not delay in fulfilling it. He has no pleasure in fools; fulfill your vow." Jesus reaffirms this when he calls his followers simply to let their yes be yes, and their no be no (Matthew 5:37). The Apostle Paul, addressing the Corinthian Christians, declares: "When I planned this [visit], did I do it lightly? Or do I make my plans in a worldly manner so that in the same breath I say, 'Yes, yes' and 'No, no'?" (2 Corinthians 1:17).

Two disciples who commit themselves to one another before God in marriage have quite a different attitude than others in our society who take vows easily and flippantly. In this day of the prenuptial agreement and easy separation, when one out of two marriages end in divorce, when broken families have become the norm rather than the exception, a Christian marriage is like a light in a dark world. As a Christian woman who is about to be married, you must recognize this difference and be prepared to truly "take this man, until death separates you." Christians cannot enter into a marriage without considering first that their ultimate commitment is to God, and that the purpose of this marriage is to glorify God. Anything less than this attitude is a denial of the first and most important vow that you have made—that Jesus is your Lord.

Not only do you enter the marriage with this disciple's mindset, but you begin preparations for the wedding with this mindset as well. With Jesus as your Lord, how can you prepare for your special day in a way that will please and bring glory to God? The following chapters of this book will give you many helpful and practical guidelines for your preparations. However, even the best of suggestions will not help you to plan a fantastic wedding if your heart is not connected with God and your mind is not spiritual. This is a time in your life you will remember always. Make it great!

ENJOY

One of the most important things to remember is this: ENJOY! Too many brides-to-be get so caught up in the details of planning a wedding that it becomes an ordeal, a chore. Preparing for a wedding is supposed to be fun! It's a time to dream together with your fiancé, to share special times with Christian friends and families. It's a time you are able to use all your creative capabilities, to choose your favorite colors and styles and flowers and music—all the things that represent the best of you and your future husband. Whether you are planning a large extravaganza of a wedding or a smaller more intimate gathering, the beauty of the wedding is that it is a celebration of your love for one another and your love for God. Decide right away that this time of planning and preparing will be a time of joy, not a time to be frantic or anxious. Later, when you reminisce about it, will the thoughts bring a smile to your face?

EXPECT

Another thing to remember may seem contradictory to what we've just said, but it really isn't. That is: EXPECT that not everything will be just perfect! This is not a statement of doom, but a reminder to have realistic expectations. Many brides get so disappointed about little things that go wrong that they are unable to enjoy the preparations for their weddings. Yes, someone's dress might be too small. Yes, some relative might get her feelings hurt. Yes, the colors of the flowers might be a shade off. Yes, the best man might even forget the ring! How will you handle these small disappointments? Your peace of mind and patience are crucial during this time. It's a wise bride who can remember the big picture and know that even if some things don't go exactly as planned, you can still be husband and wife! Every wedding that I have been a part of (and there have been MANY) has had at least one thing go wrong, but the marriage still took place, and in most instances the bride and groom were able to look at the problems with a humorous eye.

One situation in particular comes to my mind: The big day arrived, the bride and bridesmaids were ready and waiting for the photographer. . .and waiting, and waiting. Finally, the bride called the photographer to discover that he had written down the wrong date and was unable to come to take pictures. This calm bride promptly found a friend with a camera, got some pictures taken and went on with the wedding. The photographs may not be the most professional, but at least they show a happy and content couple who didn't allow a slip-up to ruin their special day! These types of difficulties can train you to handle other problems later in married life. Impress your future husband with your tranquility and gentleness in the midst of trying circumstances. Even better than that—impress God!

EXPRESS

As you approach your wedding day, EXPRESS your love and gratitude. Don't forget to make this a special time for the groom!

Most of us, from the time we were young girls, have been planning a wedding. We had it all planned out, except for one thing: the man! Some women, in preparing for their marriage, do the same thing: they leave out the man! They know what they want and how they want to do it, and neglect to make sure this is what their fellows have in mind!

Not all men are the same. Some want to be very involved in all the intricacies of the wedding plans, others would be glad to leave it up to you; just tell them when to do what! You must know what expectations your fiancé has and do your best to fulfill them. In the meantime, keep letting him know of your love for him and your excitement to be his wife. Make him confident that your happiness is not just in planning the wedding of your dreams, but in marrying the man of your dreams!

Express your love to your friends in the church for the help they are giving you. It's so easy to take this help for granted. Every service, suggestion, gift or advice should be received with a thankful heart. Send thank-you notes. If someone has been extremely helpful, take them out for lunch to show your appreciation. Of course, when there is a fee for a service, give it gladly, not begrudgingly. Don't have a "you owe it to me" attitude.

Express your love to your families during this special time. Weddings are a time of overflowing emotions! For your parents, it may be a time of mixed feelings to see their little girl truly grown up and with a life of her own. Be understanding, knowing you may feel the same some day! If your family situation is one of friction or difficulty, or if there is some antagonism regarding the marriage, it can be extremely difficult. Your duty is to remain a righteous woman with love and compassion towards all. Do your best to keep peace, and to make this a time for the family to see the power of God in your life. We all know of families who have been so impacted by Christian weddings that they have become Christians themselves!

Above all, express your love to God as you prepare for marriage. Remember that it is by the grace of God that you have this relationship. Even though this is a very busy time, don't neglect prayer or Bible study. Remember that God is your first love! Your relationship with him is of utmost importance and can't be shoved aside until after the honeymoon!

In the weeks and months to follow, you will be meeting all kinds of people: the baker, the florist, the seamstress. . .the list is endless. Even before the big day, you will be making an impression. These people will see the real you. What will they say about you? Will they see a difference in you? Will they see the love of Christ in your heart? Will they hear about your gratitude for your church, your relationships? Will they know about the blessings you have? Will they know that you are deeply in love with your fiancé, but that the one you love the most is God? It's up to you. As you prepare to take your vows of marriage, don't forget your first vow, the most important vow . . .the vow of "JESUS IS LORD!"

Brides of Christ
PLAY

In 1990 Marcia Lamb wrote a two-act play depicting the different personality types as they began to plan their weddings. The title was "Brides of Christ" and an exerpt is included here with thanks to Marcia for allowing us to use it. At the beginning of Act 2, a women's ministry leader, Zona, has just drifted to sleep after attending a wedding rehearsal for Bunnie Sue and her fiancé. She begins to dream that she has been divinely appointed as the wedding coordinator for the church, and in her dream she meets with each bride to counsel her about the impending wedding.

As you read and laugh, look for a caricature of yourself. With which of the following brides do you most identify?

First Zona prays before she goes to bed, reflecting on the night and its happenings:

"...and Lord, thank you for pulling off Bunnie Sue's wedding rehearsal this evening. I pray that Bunnie Sue, Mrs. Jones, Mary Beth and Grandpa Frank's illnesses were due to nerves and not to food poisoning. Lord, please forgive the bridesmaids for what they're about to wear tomorrow, for they knew not what they looked like till tonight. And Lord, bless dear sister Smith for staying up all night sewing extra lace on the bodices. God, I pray that Mr. and Mrs. Jones will show up at the wedding tomorrow, they seemed a bit upset after the sharing tonight. Please help Bunnie Sue forgive her old roommates for their sharing so ... uh ... well ...vigorously tonight about her drug dealings before she became a Christian. Her mother looked a little upset. Oh my, it's 2:00 a.m.! Be with my husband as he is counseling Freddie tonight about their honeymoon. (to herself) Freddie was so cute tonight when he said, 'Now can we have the big talk?' I'm so glad Bunnie Sue didn't need one of those talks. (shudders) She's already lived with three men. Well, Lord, this is good night. Amen." (She sleeps.)

The angel, Giddy Ann, enters via a dream and wakes her up to give her the charge of being the church wedding coordinator. She begins to bring in the brides one at a time to be counseled by Zona:

MISS CINDY RELLA

Zona: Tell me about your plans, Cindy.

Cindy: It'll be wonderful. I'll be there and so will Johnny. We'll have it in a quaint little church in the woods. It will be by a lake with swans, and the bridal party will float up to the church on a gondola with sixteen violins playing in the background. After the outdoor reception, hundreds of guests will throw rose petals as Johnny and I ride off in our carriage.

Zona: It sounds beautiful. Where did you find such a place?

Cindy: Oh, we're still looking for it—but I know we'll find it.

Zona: So you'll be having a summer wedding then?

Cindy: Oh no! It's this month!

Zona: This month? Why it could be snowing! Maybe you should consider something a little more practical. Besides, you've only got weeks to prepare. We've got work to do.

Cindy: It'll be fine. It'll work out. It'll be beautiful!
        (She walks off in a daze.)

Zona: She doesn't need a counselor. She needs a fairy godmother.

11

MISS THUSLAH

Miss T: All right, who's in charge here? (She carries a huge
          organizer, looks very business-like.) I got engaged last
          night, although I was still in bed by 10:30. I'll be getting
          married in six months, twenty days and eight hours from
          now and I want to get started on this wedding. I was told
          I needed to talk to you.

Zona: Well, congratulations! First, we should talk about a few
          things such as your wedding party and location.

Miss T: I've already taken care of all that. I've had my brides-
          maids on alert for seven years. I called the church
          to confirm my penciled-in date and the caterer is notified.

Zona: My, you are prepared. What does your fiancé think
          about all of this?

Miss T: Look! I've had this wedding planned for years and no
          one is going to change it! I have the patterns for the
          bridesmaids' dresses. . .although they could use a little
          modernizing. The material is bought. . .though I might
          need to get a few more yards for Bertha; she's had three
          kids and has added a few pounds since I asked her. I
          have a count-down calendar in detail. ..the invitations,
          the gift registry, the rehearsal, the limo service, dry-
          cleaners for my dress, environmentally correct bird seed,
          the flowers, the pew bows. . .

Zona: I'm very impressed, Miss Thuslah, but I don't see any
          place (looks at calendar) in your schedule for you and
          your fiancé to work together on your wedding, let alone
          your relationship.

Miss T: This is MY wedding. I'm sure Harold will be happy when I tell him what we're going to do. Good day.

MISS WORLD

Miss W: My last name is World. My first name is Lee. By coincidence I'm marrying this darling little man named Mr. Lee. Rather than being called Lee Lee, I'm retaining my maiden name. So I will be Lee World Lee.

Zona: (to angel) Uh oh, I think we are in trouble. (to Miss World) Shall we proceed?

Miss W: Yes, Precious, I want you to plan me a glorious formal, truly traditional wedding and reception. Spare no expense. I want the best of everything for my family and friends to see. . .uh. . .I mean to enjoy.

Zona: If you want me to plan it, we need to talk budgets.

Miss W: Budgets, smudgets. You sound like my father. We'll worry about that after the wedding. Besides, aren't the people in the church supposed to provide for each other? So, what we can't afford, the church people can do for us.

Zona: So you haven't really done much planning or saving?

Miss W: Well, I have bought my dress and all my trousseau. Here's a picture of it.

Zona: Oh, a picture of your negligee (shocked!). Where's your wedding dress?

Miss W: That *is* my wedding dress. Well, it's obvious that you don't know what's in.

Zona: I'm not worried about what's in—but what's left out.
          (to angel) I don't think the bride will be the only one
          blushing at this wedding.

PRUDENCE PANIC

P. Panic:(comes in like a tornado, dropping papers, flustered and
          fluttering about how much she has to do and no time to
          do it. She's oblivious to angel and Zona.) Rice bags, pew
          bows, tuxedos, dress hemmed. (After a few minutes of
          her fluttering and fretting. . .)

Zona: I'm Zona. May I help you?

P. Panic:Oh no! I couldn't possible bother you with my wedding.
          Oh no. Thank you for offering though. (leaves mutter
          ing) How am I ever going to get all this done?

Zona: (to angel) This is hard. Why do I have to deal with all
          these difficult brides? They're so self-willed and selfish.
          What can I possibly do to change their attitudes?

MISS MISTY FIED

Zona: Okay. Let's see what you've already decided to do.

Misty: Well, I. . .uh. . .can't decide. . .

Zona: Finally an open one!

Misty: I can't decide who to have in my wedding. You see, my
          fiancé Steve wants me to cut back, but I don't know who
          to cut out. I mean (sniffling) they're all so special to me.
          My three sisters, his two sisters, my ministry leader, my
          discipleship partner and all the Bible talk members.

They are so close to me. Then there is my best friend in kindergarten, my Girl Scout leader and my piano teacher. Then there's that really open woman I met yesterday.

Zona: Wait a minute! How many people are you asking?

Misty: Twenty.

Zona: That's a bit unreasonable. Let's try to cut back.

Misty: But I can't decide. I know, let's put the names in a hat and you draw them out! Then I won't have to hurt anyone's feelings.

Zona: Hold it! You can't choose people that way. Let's look at this list. Sisters. . .okay. Your piano teacher. . .are you really close to her?

Misty: Well, actually, I haven't seen her in years. But she made an impact on my life and I thought it would mean a lot to her for me to ask her. I think she is probably still alive.

Zona: Okay, okay, let's work on this a little later. What about the dresses, color scheme, music and food?

Misty: All the women in my family wear my grandmother's wedding dress. It's kind of a greenish, off-white now. Colors? Well, blue is Steve's favorite color, green is my mother's favorite and orange is his mother's favorite color. My sisters refuse to wear "warm" colors and Daddy says he likes his little girls in purples. I just can't decide because I want everyone to be happy. Music and food is easy. Steve would want country-western music and a barbecue after. He said I could choose pork or beef.

Zona: But, Misty, what are your favorite things?

Misty: I don't know, what do you think they should be?
        Whatever you think is fine with me.

Zona: Before we go on, do you have any strong personal
        feelings about what you want in your wedding?

Misty: Oh, yes! Ever since I was a little girl, I promised my
        dearest, closest friend that she would be in my wedding.
        But Steve objects because of his allergies.

Zona: That seems reasonable to have your best friend in your
        wedding.

Misty: Well, I know she's kind of sickly and old, but I thought
        I could carry her myself in a basket with flowers and
        ribbons. It'll be beautiful. (sniffs pitifully)

Zona: Wait a minute! You want to carry a sick old woman
        down the aisle in a basket?

Misty: No, not a woman. My cat, Patches!

RUBY STONE AND HER MOTHER MILLIE STONE

Ruby: I'm so glad to meet you, Zona. I really appreciate your
        helping us with our wedding. I want it to be as special
        and unique as our love, yet simple and reasonable so we
        won't be burdened financially. I wanted to get your
        advice on some of our choices because we really do want
        to bring God glory through this wedding.

Zona: (to angel) Now this is more like it. (to Ruby) This is
        wonderful. I'm sure I can help you.

16

Millie: (rushes in abruptly) There you are, Ruby. I flew all the way out here to make sure this wedding is done right. (to Zona) Millie's my name, Millie Stone. I'm Ruby's mother. Now, see here, I want none of this nonsense that I've been hearing over the phone. (starts crying) It's bad enough that you broke dear great-aunt Ethel's heart by not asking her to sing at your wedding, but then you go and choose the wrong color scheme. You know I clash with pink. (Millie bumps Ruby out of her chair.) Now let's get this mess straightened out!

        (Fade out)

Zona: (crying out to God) Oh, please! I can't do this! I don't know how to help these brides. They're hopeless! Please, make me the kingdom travel agent or anything but this. (Zona crawls into bed, pulling the covers over her head.)

        (Pause)

Angel: Zona, Zona, wake up! He's here! The bridegroom is here!

Zona: Oh, no! You mean I have to deal with him too?

Angel: Zona, when you focus on the bridegroom, you'll know what to teach the brides. You will have wisdom, courage and love. They will be radiant because of him.

Zona: Bring me to him, please.

Voice: (majestically reads from off stage) ". . .Christ loved the church and gave himself up for her to make her holy, cleansing her by the washing with water through the word, and to present her to himself as a radiant church,

17

without stain or wrinkle or any other blemish, but holy
and blameless" (Ephesians 5:25-27). ". . .Hallelujah! For
our Lord God Almighty reigns. Let us rejoice and be
glad and give him glory! For the wedding of the Lamb
has come and his bride has made herself ready. Fine
linen, bright and clean, was given her to wear. . . .
'Blessed are those who are invited to the wedding supper
of the Lamb!'. . .These are the true words of God"
(Revelation19:6-9).

(Fade out)

END

PLANS

2

BEFORE WE GET STARTED

Did you see yourself in any of the brides whom Zona encountered? Are you more like Cindy Rella or maybe like Misty Fied? It's good to laugh. It's also good to learn about yourself as you approach this important time in your life. Each personality type has specific temptations in planning and struggling with decisions. Women of all personality types need to stay close to God so their weddings will bring glory to him and encourage other people.

The next nine chapters will give you direction and information for planning your wedding, reception and honeymoon. Remember, though, that your wedding is YOURS—it is for you and your fiancé. An individual wedding. One that reflects your lives, your unique talents and desires. As you proceed with your plans, some people who are well-meaning, although misinformed, may tell you how you should do your wedding. They may try to tell you what type of wedding is appropriate. They may even indicate that you are doing something "wrong" just because you are doing something different. According to Emily Post, weddings are a time for individuality and there are no true absolutes. The wedding ceremony that I include is only a basic guideline. You can vary it in many ways. But do get advice from a professional who can tell you if your plans are feasible.

This is among the most special times in your life. Be sensitive to family desires, but do not compromise any part that you may later regret. In planning, decide which parts are crucial to you and which ones are optional.

Take time to enjoy your engagement and pray that you will be calm and relaxed on your wedding day so that you can cherish every moment of it. God will grant you the desire of your heart.

Make sure to have special, non-wedding-oriented time with your fiancé since the time will fly by faster than you can imagine.

If you take the time at first to pay attention to detail, you will be able to enjoy your engagement and ceremony in an incredible way.

With love in Christ,

Nancy Poe Orr
Professional Wedding Consultant
Wedding Musician

Chapter 1

DECIDING WHAT YOU WANT

Look around at a wedding. Who are the people paying the most attention to all the details? Usually, the singles who are looking forward to being married themselves. They count the bridesmaids. They listen carefully to the words of the songs. They make mental notes as the bride and groom exchange their personal vows. You have probably done this more than once yourself and so, more than likely, you already have some pretty definite ideas of what you want your wedding to be.

Beautiful, impacting weddings don't just happen on the wing of a wish. The need is to pray and plan—the two most important ingredients in a joyous and encouraging wedding experience.

The following are several practicals to keep in mind as you decide what you want in the wedding of your dreams:

1. Remember that your wedding may be the only chance for some people to hear the message about Jesus. You want it to reflect your life and your beliefs—not just your artistic and aesthetic desires and abilities.

2. It is important to force yourself to think in details—not just sweeping "wouldn't it be beautiful..." ideas. Some will more naturally do this, but the same organized ones might also forget to rely on God. Determine that you will keep the right balance of prayer and planning. Pray over every detail. Be specific in your prayers. God is a faithful God and delights in granting us the desires of our hearts.

3. A good exercise is to visualize your wedding from the time that the doors open to the guests until the last guest leaves for the reception. Write down the details that you would like in a loose-leaf notebook which you use exclusively for your wedding or use the planning pages in PART 3 of this book. This part includes

both checklists and blank pages. Repeat the exercise with the rehearsal dinner and the reception.

4. Traditionally, the bride and her family make all decisions about the wedding and the reception, and the groom and his family take care of the rehearsal dinner. However, etiquette now allows for joint decisions between the bride and the groom, especially since many brides have been financially independent for some time before their wedding. In a Christian wedding there are plenty of opportunities for everyone to work together as a team, and specifically for you to practice cooperation with your future marriage partner. Make sure you are not making independent decisions about your (plural) wedding.

5. Weddings do not have to be rushed or nerve-wracking. Most of the details in my wedding were worked out in our first month of engagement as I went about my daily life. What a great opportunity it was for sharing my faith. Everyone is happy to talk with a prospective bride! My husband studied the Bible with one of his best men, and the last week before the wedding he made the decision to become a disciple of Jesus. Planning ahead helps you to stay spiritually focused and allows you to make the most impact on others.

Together with your fiancé, consider the various aspects of the pre-wedding activities, the ceremony itself, the desired ambience and the reception. The more carefully you formulate your plans, the better you will be able to carry them out.

Just remember—take time for your relationship with God, your fiancé, family and friends. Don't put everyone on a back burner as you plan your wedding. If you keep your spiritual perspective, you will be able both to envision your wedding and to enjoy your life.

Chapter 2

PLANNING YOUR BUDGET

efore you begin the actual planning of your wedding, it is important to know how much money you will have to work with. An average wedding will cost anywhere from $10,000 to $20,000 and up (depending, of course, on the region in which you live). Included in this cost is not only the ceremony and reception, but also the honeymoon and start-up living expenses (first and last month's rent). Couples sometimes plan only for the ceremony and reception and end up going into debt for the honeymoon and other starting costs. It is possible to have a very nice wedding for under $5,000, but you must plan very carefully. I encourage couples to keep costs down unless their families are paying for and want a more expensive wedding. Many families plan for years for their daughter's wedding by putting aside money in special accounts. On the other hand, many brides and grooms are financially independent from their families and may not have a large amount of money on hand.

SO WHERE DO YOU BEGIN?

1. Determine your own financial situation. Consider all of your current bills and financial responsibilities and how much you can raise or save for your wedding. It is probably a good idea to be a bit conservative in your budgeting. Plan for the worst financial scenario and hope and pray for the best.

2. Have your fiancé do the same.

3. Ask your families how much they would like to contribute. Some families may wish to pay for the entire wedding. Others may not be able to.

A BIT OF CAUTION

Since financial responsibility is characteristic of a disciple, don't go into debt with your wedding. Strive to please God in your plans and be wise. The fewer added financial stresses that you have as newlyweds, the better off you will be. Decide that you will not do what you cannot afford to do. A simple wedding can be beautiful and meaningful.

After considering the three beginning steps, you should have a pretty good idea of where you stand financially. Now you can more accurately determine what type of wedding you are able to have.

THE BREAKDOWN

The bride's (or her family's) budget should include:

1. Wedding dress and alterations (including shoes, slip, veil, bra, two pairs pantyhose, jewelry) $200-$3000
2. Building rental for wedding and/or reception (including custo dial costs, etc.) $200-$500
3. Reception costs (including birdseed, decorations, garter, bag or basket for cards, table linens, etc.) $500-$15,000
4. Wedding cake (include cake knife and server, glasses for bride and groom, cutting fee for some reception areas) $1-$4 per person
5. Flowers (genuine, dried or silk) $200-$2000
     —building decorations
     —bridesmaids, flower girl, groom, groomsmen, ministers, fathers, ring bearers
     —pew bows
     —include the runner, candelabra, candles, ring bearer's pillow
     —reception flowers, bouquet to toss

6. Groom's wedding ring $60-$300
7. Housing for out-of-town guests
8. Hospitality baskets for out-of-town guests

9. Initial start-up living costs (including first and last month's rent)
10. Fees for minister, musicians, sound technicians, equipment rental, photographer, videographer
11. Bride's trousseau
12. Invitations (with two stamps for each), thank-you cards and stamps
13. Bridal luncheon (to honor bridesmaids)
14. Gifts for the wedding party
15. Gift for the groom

The groom's (or his family's) budget should include:

1. Honeymoon $1000-$6000
2. Bride's bouquet, mother's flowers $100-$300
3. Bride's wedding ring $50-$200
4. Initial start-up living costs
5. Rental of tuxedo, shoes, etc. $80-$100
6. Rental of tuxedo for minister (optional: can wear dark suit)
7. Rehearsal dinner (including the place, music, food, etc.)
8. Gifts for wedding party
9. Gift for the bride

MAKING GOOD DECISIONS

There may be many costs that you haven't even thought of. But, thankfully, there are ways to cut these costs. For example, bridal salons and even some department stores often have incredible deals on dresses for the bride and for the entire wedding party. Check the yellow pages for wedding consignment shops. You can find beautiful dresses—worn only once—at half of the original cost. Talk to other brides to find out how they were able to cut costs without cutting corners on quality. (Two pages are included in PART 3 for you to jot down money-saving ideas that you discover.)

Also, seek advice from professionals. A professional may be able to suggest a less expensive way to get what you want or to achieve the effect you would like. They will also help you to know if your budgeting is realistic. If you have budgeted $50 for music, it is probably not realistic to think that you could have the Julliard String Quartet play for the ceremony—unless they are your best friends and are offering their services as a gift.

Take the time to attend some weddings and note what you like and don't like. Then talk with the newlyweds (after their honeymoon) whose weddings you particularly liked. Learning from them could save you both time and money.

Comparison shop for florists, photographers, caterers, etc.

Don't be afraid to bargain with people. Most people in the wedding business can pare their prices somewhat.

Go to bridal shows. In general, take the time to find out what is available for what price before you make any decisions. Your engagement is a wonderful opportunity to meet many people from different walks of life and to share your joy and gratitude during such a happy time in your life. Everyone loves to talk to a bride and groom about their wedding plans. Take advantage of the opportunity to be light and leaven in situations you will probably never be in again.

Finally, take control of the financial planning of your wedding. Don't let it take control of you.

(see budget forms in Part 3)

Chapter 3

MAKING PRELIMINARY DECISIONS

Now that you are spiritually focused and have spent time visualizing the various details of your wedding, it is time to begin the actual legwork. With so many details to be taken care of, this aspect could become overwhelming. Without a sense of direction, you could find yourself scattered everywhere and accomplishing little. Now is the time to take hold of your wedding plans and to begin with a clear sense of purpose and focus as you approach one of the most memorable and important days of your life.

Where do you start? By now, you have determined your overall budget, so you can begin the plans by making six fundamental decisions:

1. Set a date for the wedding.
To do this, you will need to be mindful of both families and their schedules and obligations. It is wise to plan an engagement that is no shorter than three-and-a-half months. It takes at least that long for a wedding gown to be ready. An ideal length of time for an engagement is six months.

2. Decide on your bridal party and ask them.
It is a great honor to be asked to be a bridesmaid or a groomsman. The people you choose should be close friends, family members and future in-laws. Ministry leaders suggest that although having several attendants shows the abundance of your close relationships, you should not have so many that the role is no longer special.

3. Find a facility for the ceremony. As you look, ask these questions:

   a. Is the building available on___date at___time?
   b. Can we use our own minister?
   c. What is the seating capacity? (Most open weddings have an attendance of 150-200)
   d. What rental fees are included? (custodian, rehearsal time)
   e. Do you allow open flame (candles)?
   f. Are there facilities for a reception? (if desired)
   g. Can we have our own musicians and/or sound equipment? (Some churches require that you use their organist)

4. Select bridal gown and headpiece.

There are many inexpensive options for this. You can have a gown made, borrow one, or buy one at a consignment shop or at a wholesale warehouse. Shop around, but leave yourself at least three months for the fittings. And if you hire a seamstress, check references.

5. Select wedding colors and choose dresses for wedding party.

When selecting the dresses, keep in mind two things: modesty and price. Don't put any of your bridesmaids in the postion of having to either go against her conscience or ask you to totally change your plans. Showing cleavage or too much skin is not in good taste. (Keep this in mind when choosing your own dress too.) Also take into account the size and build of the women you have chosen. A dress that would be appropriate on a flat-chested woman might not be appropriate at all on a more amply endowed woman. Think ahead and get advice.

As for the price of the dress, your bridesmaids are honored to be part of your wedding and want to be able to buy what you have chosen. Be sensitive to their budgets—buying dresses that cost $100 or more, can be a real hardship for women who are committed to living sacrificially. Keep in mind also that they will need to buy shoes, pantyhose and other accessories to complete the outfit. Of course, selecting a dress that they can wear again is a very thoughtful gesture.

6. Decide on type of reception and find a place.

As you begin your hunt for a reception facility, you will discover that some places are booked very far in advance. Many people have one- to two-year engagements. Even six months in advance is considered short notice by some function halls.

After making these six major decisions, you will still have myriad other details to consider, but you will be well on your way to a well-planned and organized wedding day—one that will bring glory to God. Making these decisions will help you move ahead in planning and working together with your family and fiancé to make your dream a reality.

Chapter 4

CONSIDERING PROFESSIONALS

hy should I hire professionals when I have my good friends, Dick and Jane, who have offered to sing, play, coordinate, and even bake the cake—all for free? A caricature? An exaggeration? Yes, but it makes the point. Sometimes offers to help are offers you should refuse.

CONSIDER A PROFESSIONAL WEDDING COORDINATOR

Your friends will be an awesome help and support. You will be able to delegate many specifics to responsible friends who will lighten your load. Before enlisting someone to help you, first consider her talents and experience. For a novice, coordinating a wedding can be frustrating or even totally overwhelming. If you ask a friend with little wedding experience to coordinate yours, you may soon find yourself having to ask an experienced person to step in and take the reins from her.

If your car were to break down, would you go to one of your friends to fix it? Probably not, unless he is a car mechanic (official or unofficial). So, why expect someone who is not a qualified wedding professional to show you how to put your wedding together? Set yourself and everyone else up for success. Get experienced help from the start.

CHOOSING OTHER PROFESSIONALS

Remember, your wedding is one of the most important days of your life. Whatever memories you create are the memories you will have, and the pictures and videos you have taken are the ones you will have—for the rest of your life. As Christians, we strive to do everything excellently. A note of balance: Even with carefully chosen professionals, things can still go wrong. There is never a guarantee that everything will run smoothly—no matter how important the occasion. The help of an experienced professional does, however, go a long way on a day when all kinds of mishaps could (and invariably do) occur. A professional not only has the knowledge and the expertise to handle most things that arise, but he or she also has the ability to keep cool and to keep everyone else cool. When it's all over, you may not even know that anything challenging happened. Remember, though, that your life and your marital happiness do not depend on a flawless marriage ceremony and reception. Just do your best. Plan and pray.

In selecting people to work with your wedding, always check credentials. Even Christians may not have an accurate assessment of their abilities. A good test with Christians is to ask for references—both those who know them well and those who don't. If they are good at what they do, they will have been called upon by many others. (Note that when I use the term "professional," I refer to those who have professional experience and ability. This particular expertise may not be their sole area of employment.)

Try to avoid situations like the following:

a. A brother taking a photography class may with a good heart assure you that he can take awesome pictures. No problem! But when he gets to the church with a skylight   roof on a cloudy day with the wrong speed film, both of you will be disappointed.

b. A sister who is a great cook may be positive that she can fix you a beautiful four-tiered wedding cake. After all, she made a Wonder Woman cake for her niece and a Barney cake for her son.

Need I say more? Check references. Look at portfolios. Watch videos. Get tapes. Go to a wedding he or she is doing. Talk with newlyweds who chose their services (after the honeymoon). Pray and make a wise choice. Then do not worry about it.

SPECIFIC PROFESSIONALS NEEDED

1. Minister(s) to officiate. (Pay the minister as you would pay any other professional.)

2. Coordinator or caterer for reception.

3. Sound technician (including equipment rental).

4. Musician(s) for wedding and sometimes for rehearsal dinner or reception.

5. Florist.

6. Seamstress for dress fittings for yourself and bridesmaids.

7. Tuxedo rental shop.

8. Song leader for congregational songs. (This person does not need to be a professional, but he should be consistent at pitching a song under pressure. Most of us have been to weddings where "O Lord, Our Lord" was sung up in the rafters.)

AFTER CHOOSING YOUR PROFESSIONALS

Be sure to remember the following:

1. **Ask a lot of questions.** Do not apologize for doing so. They may do weddings everyday, but you don't do yours everyday.

2. **Do not assume anything about fees.** Ask about hidden costs. "Is this included in your fee?" "Will you charge for this service?" Don't assume that everyone is being honest and up-front if you do not know their lives. Even between Christians, misunderstandings and miscommunications can occur. The person who is more

experienced may assume that the other knows what is standard practice; the less experienced person may assume she is being told every detail. Be specific.

3. Get any agreement in writing.
If they balk at a written agreement, balk at using them.

After you have done your best to make responsible, spiritual decisions, delegate and let go. You cannot carry around with you the responsibility for executing every detail yourself. Remember, that's why you have chosen others to help you. Now, let them do it.

Chapter 5

PLANNING THE CEREMONY

Everything that you are doing—all of the preparations, all of the planning, all of the advice—culminates in the wedding ceremony. Up until now, we have spent a great deal of time on the details and the how-to's. Now it is time to think about the ceremony itself.

We will break it into three parts:

1. The rehearsal and rehearsal dinner
2. The wedding
3. The reception

The reception will be covered in the next chapter, but because the rehearsal and rehearsal dinner are so key to the atmosphere of the wedding day, they will be included in this chapter.

A SUCCESSFUL REHEARSAL

The minister is responsible for running a smooth rehearsal *(see Part 3)*, but by considering the following suggestions, the bride and groom can help to ensure a smoother one.

1. Make sure you communicate clearly with all who need to attend the rehearsal—the wedding party, the ceremony coordinator, and your families. If any part of your ceremony is highly unusual, you may wish to ask the videographer or a head musician to come as well.

2. Ask all of the bridesmaids to bring their wedding shoes to the rehearsal. This actually serves two purposes. It more accurately

shows the bridesmaids' heights, and it also gives them a chance to scuff up the soles of their shoes. Hopefully this will prevent their skating down the aisle the next day.

3. Bring masking tape to mark the floor where each member of the bridal party is to stand. This is so they can remember to put their feet where you so carefully positioned them the night before. (Note: You may wish to speak with the custodian and ask that he not remove the tape in his zeal to have a spotless building for the ceremony.)

4. If you are using candles in your ceremony, you should bring two boxes of kitchen matches and a cigarette lighter. Bring these to the rehearsal because you might forget them amidst the wedding day jitters. Light the candles briefly during the rehearsal evening to ensure easier lighting the next day. We've all watched in strained silence as distraught candlelighters have tried unsuccessfully to light a new wick.

5. Let the minister know whether you would prefer to face him or to face the audience during the ceremony. Also make it clear whether you want the wedding party to be placed as couples or with men on one side and women on the other.

THE REHEARSAL DINNER

Even though the groom and his parents traditionally pay for the rehearsal dinner, the engaged couple sets the tone and the atmosphere. This dinner is an opportunity for the bride and the groom to honor the wedding party and the families.

Since your families and friends have done so much to bring you to this point in your lives, this is a wonderful opportunity to thank them in special ways. Typically, this is a time when you and your fiancé can pour out your hearts in gratitude for these special people and share with others why you love and appreciate them. It is during this time that the bride and groom often give each member of the wedding party a small gift as a memento of the wedding. Some brides may prefer, though, to give the bridesmaids their gifts during a bridesmaids' luncheon.

Another idea which has become a custom among many Christians is to have a time when people in the families or in the bridal party can share about the bride and the groom. You might want to remind brothers and sisters to be sensitive and aware of your families in their sharing. Let them know to be discrete about your pre-Christian days and to make sure your families have ample opportunity to share. **Be sure to set a specific ending time for the sharing.** You might ask specific people ahead of time to share so you can keep the time from going too long.

You are free to add any personal touches, such as a special song, to create the atmosphere that you desire. Again, though, remember to be mindful of the time. The rehearsal dinner precedes the wedding day which begins with early-morning preparations.

As in any other aspect of your wedding, spend time planning, dreaming, preparing and praying about a dinner that will impact the hearts and the lives of all who attend.

THE CEREMONY

When planning the wedding ceremony, consider tradition and etiquette, but don't be afraid to insert your own stamp of originality. There are many ways to individualize a wedding.

If you are from a particular ethnic background, you may wish your wedding to reflect this. You could include different customs from your culture in the ceremony. You can also create a unique atmosphere by including pictures, cards or other things that draw the wedding guests into your cultural background.

The ways in which ceremonies can be customized are as numerous as the couples who get married. As you plan, think creatively about ways to make your ceremony unique and special. But, if tradition is very important to you, have it be as traditional as you like. Remember, your wedding is your wedding and you and your fiancé will make the final decisions in the planning. It should reflect you, not someone else.

THE BASIC CEREMONY

Prelude *(20–30 minutes of background music)*
Guests are seated during this time by the groomsmen. You do not need to select every piece of music for this portion of the wedding, but it is helpful to decide on the mood—i.e. worshipful, joyous, mellow, etc. You should decide what instrument(s) will be playing and if you want a vocalist for one or two songs.

Lighting of candelabra *(if used)* - toward end of prelude

Seating of mothers *(can include grandmothers, special aunts, etc.)* Note: Bride's mother is seated last.

Mothers light candles—two candles that are later used to light unity candle *(optional)*

Entrance of groom, best man, minister(s)

Entrance of other groomsmen, unless they are escorting bridesmaids down the aisle

Bridesmaids' processional

Runner rolled out *(optional)*

Ring bearer and flower girl *(optional)*
Note: If preferred, runner can be rolled out after ring bearer and flower girl.

Bridal processional *(usually escorted by father or another man)*

Congregational hymn and/or prayer *(optional)*

Giving away the bride

Sermonette

Personal sharing by minister or friend *(optional)*

Vows *(personal and/or traditional)*

Unity candle *(optional)*

Rings

Pronouncement

Recessional
 Bride and groom
 Ring bearer and flower girl
 Ushers escorting bridesmaids
 Bride's mother *(escorted by usher)* and other women
  from the bride's family who were seated during the
  ceremony
 Groom's mother *(escorted by usher)* and other women
  from groom's family who were seated during the
  ceremony
 note: last in, first out

Chapter 6

PLANNING THE RECEPTION

The reception is where most of your wedding expenses will be incurred; it requires careful and thoughtful planning. But it is not just a social event—this is where you begin your new life together. Think about the tone and atmosphere you want to set so that your first hours of being married will be an encouragement to you and to others.

QUESTIONS TO ASK YOURSELF

1. How much money do I have budgeted for the reception?
The amount budgeted should include:
   a. Cake
   b. Food and beverages
   c. The facility
   d. Music (if any)
   e. Decor
   f. Table linens, chairs, tables, silverware
   g. Any other incidentals

2. What kind of reception do I want?
   a. Sit-down dinner
      ($15-$40 per person)
   b. Stand-up hors d'oeuvres
      ($6-$15 per person)
   c. Cake and light refreshments only
      ($2-$4 per person)

3. Do I want an open or a closed reception?

4. If by invitation only, how many people would I invite?

5. Do I want dancing?
    a. Hiring a band can run $800-$2000 for 3-4 hours
    b. Hiring a disc jockey can run $200-$500

6. How much do I want to spend on the cake?

7. What kind of atmosphere do I want?
    a. Restaurant, function hall or hotel
       (These places usually have package deals.)
    b. Outdoor reception
       (You would need a caterer.)
    c. The church reception hall
       (Again, you would need a caterer.)

8. How much do I want to spend on decorations?
Many people use the bridal and bridesmaids' bouquets to decorate the reception. During some seasons, such as Christmas and Easter, different facilities may already have flower arrangements which you can use. Make it clear to those setting up or cleaning that you will be using the arrangements—both verbally and by placing a note by the arrangements themselves.

RESEARCHING YOUR RECEPTION

As you would for any other aspect of the wedding, shop around. This search can actually be an enjoyable adventure. Go on dates with your fiancé to different places and try their food. Check out their atmosphere. Ask what services are available and which of these are offered at an extra fee. For example, some establishments may charge a fee if you do not get your wedding cake from them.

You need to determine what you are willing to pay for the sake of convenience. If you choose to have a catering company cater your reception, be sure to find out if their fee includes plates, silverware, glasses, tables and chairs, decorations, table linens and beverages. Don't be afraid to sound ignorant. Any company who wants to serve you should be more than happy to explain their services and to answer your questions.

41

Ask for references and ask for a written contract. Don't sign on the dotted line immediately. You may feel the pressure to make quick decisions as the day rapidly approaches. Relax and take some time to decide. You can always ask them to pencil in the date and hold it for a couple of days. You may find as you drive away that ten questions or concerns pop into your head, and you will be glad that you are taking the time to think it through.

MAY I HAVE THIS DANCE?

If you are having dancing, you will, of course, need to have music. When selecting the musicians, listen to a demo tape to see if they have the sound you want. Ask for references and check them out.

After deciding on your musician(s) or disc jockey, you may wish to go over their list of music. Ask them about the typical types of comments they make while playing for receptions. This will hopefully ensure that there will be no surprises about songs or comments. Make your convictions clear to them and be specific about what you consider appropriate and inappropriate for your reception.

Ask them to tell you, in writing, exactly who will be playing or singing. It is a practice, although unethical, to send in a musician other than the one you thought you had hired. A signed contract could spare you some wedding-day aggravations.

A FINAL NOTE

Spend some time thinking about the type of atmosphere that you want, and commit it to prayer. Do you want a big celebration, a quiet, intimate time with close family and friends, a reception that celebrates God's creation (at the ocean or in a garden setting), or something in-between? Whatever it is that you want, you need to decide fairly quickly, as reception halls book up months (and sometimes a full year) in advance—especially between April and December.

When the day of your reception comes, have fun, relax and enjoy all of your relationships. Thank God for bringing together all of your family and friends and for fulfilling your dreams.

Chapter 7

WORKING WITH A TIMETABLE

J n chapter three we talked about the six most important decisions you need to make to begin your planning. These should all be taken care of in the first month of engagement, and the sooner into that month, the better. Now we come to all of those nitty-gritty details that can fluster people so much. With some organization and discipline, you can take care of these as you go about your day-to-day life.

As you plan your daily schedule, devote one hour to your wedding. If that hour is immediately after work, you can go from work to florists, to caterers, to photographers or to whomever you need to see.

The following timetable is set up assuming a three-and-a-half month engagement:

THREE MONTHS BEFORE THE WEDDING

___ Choose date and time for wedding
___ Choose professional wedding consultant (optional)
___ Choose bridal party and ask them
___ Find place to be married
___ Decide on type of reception
___ Book facility for reception
___ Book caterers
___ Order wedding gown
___ Decide wedding colors
___ Select dresses for wedding party and arrange first fittings
___ Begin working on honeymoon plans (groom's responsibility)
___ Begin gathering names (proper names) and addresses for guest list and ask both families to do the same
___ Find place for rehearsal dinner (groom's responsibility)

___ Make doctor's appointment (ob/gyn)
___ Make list of close friends who are not in bridal party and can help in other parts of wedding
___ Ask a minister to officiate at wedding
___ Order invitations, personalized napkins, announcements, thank-you cards, and other special items

TWO MONTHS BEFORE THE WEDDING

___ Select bakery
___ Arrange fittings for bridesmaids
___ Shop for gifts for bridal party
___ Make hair appointment
___ Purchase accessories for wedding dress (earrings, necklace, gloves, shoes, two pairs pantyhose, garter)
___ Buy strapless bra (if needed) and wedding gown slip and bring to fittings
___ Make first doctor's appointment and discuss birth control
___ Do something special for fiancé
___ Arrange housing for out-of-town guests
___ Purchase wedding veil
___ Get white handbag for cards and monetary gifts
___ Purchase cake top, cake knife and server, toast glasses
___ Purchase guest book and pen
___ Confer with mothers about their dresses
___ Select musicians for wedding and reception
___ Select sound technician, disc jockey, etc. for wedding and reception (if needed)
___ Select florist (bring swatch of bridesmaids' dress fabric to consultations)
___ Select photographer
___ Select videographer
___ Call church and get aisle length for runner
___ Order or buy all necessary candles and candelabra (check with church or florist)
___ Purchase two stamps per invitation and one per thank-you card

___Write invitations
___Confirm with reception facility any changes or options
___Order tuxedo and select tuxedos for groomsmen and ring bearer (groom's responsibility)
___Arrange fitting for men (groom's responsibility)
___Purchase pillow for ring bearer
___Order or make birdseed packets or make a pretty basket filled with birdseed
___Delegate responsibilities to responsible friends:

    ___ Cleaning church after wedding (3-5 people)
    ___ Cleaning rehearsal facility
    ___ Making hospitality baskets for out-of-town guests (include a personal note from you)
    ___ Bringing birdseed to reception
    ___ Attending guest-book table
    ___ Returning groom's tuxedo
    ___ Taking wedding gown to cleaners or to new home
    ___ Bringing ring bearer's pillow to wedding
    ___ Bringing glasses, cake knife and server to reception
    ___ Providing transportation for out-of-town guests
    ___ Cleaning new home before newlyweds return from honeymoon
    ___ Making meal for first night back
    ___ Returning get-away car
    ___ Taking newlyweds to airport, depot, etc.
    ___ Stand-in bride for wedding rehearsal
    ___ Wedding day coordinator (cues bridesmaids and mothers when to go down aisle, assists bride in last-minute details, assists groom, assists groomsmen with ushering, and coordinates wedding party, sound man, musicians, and photographer and/or videographer)
    ___ Select rings and arrange sizing and inscriptions
    ___ Arrange to take off last few days before wedding (as well as honeymoon time)
    ___ Arrange place for first night (groom)

___ Find a new apartment
___ Send announcement to publications (church bulletin, newspaper)

ONE MONTH BEFORE THE WEDDING

___ Start a countdown in the book of Psalms—begin with Psalm 30 or 31 and read a psalm a day, ending with Psalm 1 on **the** day
___ Continue to pray about specifics of wedding day: attitudes, weather, etc.
___ Make second hair appointment
___ Get blood tests
___ Apply for wedding license (bring results of blood tests)
___ Confirm date and time with and give maps to:
   ___   Caterer
   ___   Florist
   ___   Videographer
   ___   Sound technician
   ___   Musicians
   ___   Minister
   ___   Wedding party
   ___   Bakery
   ___   Wedding guests
___ Make doctor's appointment (only if needed)
___ Arrange wedding-day grooming appointment (facial, manicure, hair and make-up)
___ Register china, flatware and houseware preferences (offer a wide range of gift prices)
___ Shop for trousseau
___ Begin writing thank-you notes
___ Arrange last fittings for yourself and bridal party
___ Make two baskets of items to take to the ceremony:
   1.   Personal items (make-up, extra pantyhose, accessories for gown, bobby pins, etc.)
   2.   Items for rehearsal (masking tape, matches, lighter)

47

___Confirm with church or hall rehearsal time, set-up time, preparation place and any other special details (fans, etc.)

___Arrange for food (high protein food and drinks) to be in dressing room of bride, groom and wedding party (to prevent fainting)

___Confirm rehearsal dinner plans and prepare your remarks

___Pick up rings and have best man put in tuxedo pocket the night before

___Have a bridal brunch or luncheon to thank the bridesmaids for their friendship and help in the wedding plans and to confirm any last details

___Purchase or make wedding gifts for each other (bride and groom)

WEEK OF THE WEDDING

___Pick up any last-minute items

___Go over wedding with minister

___Pick up license and put it into basket of personal items for the ceremony

___Finalize last honeymoon details:

      ___   going away clothes

      ___   person in charge of car and suitcases

      ___   passports, traveler's checks, visas, etc.

      ___   any special touches for first-night room

___Spend special time with fiancé and family

___Ask women to bring wedding shoes to rehearsal

___Confirm wedding rehearsal and ceremony plans with wedding party

___Write vows (if doing personal vows)

___Write thank-you notes

___Write all checks and put in basket going to wedding

This list might seem overwhelming. However, if you take care of each detail as you go, you will find that it is not too difficult. Feel free to ask your bridesmaids to help you. Delegate as much as you would like and then check with them later to confirm that the task has been completed. Your bridesmaids are there to help you with your wedding. That is why they are called "bride's maids." They will be honored to assist you during this exciting time of your life.

If something doesn't need to be done until the last month, but you are able to do it earlier, by all means, do it. This timetable is to assist you in knowing what must absolutely be done by that time. Don't get so frazzled that you forget to spend quality time with God, your fiancé and friends. Don't get so focused on details that you forget to enjoy this special time. Continue to pray and plan—then trust that God will bless your wedding.

Chapter 8

PLANNING THE HONEYMOON

hether you are relaxing in a heart-shaped sauna in the Poconos or hiking in the Rockies, your honeymoon is a special time for you to be together. In your pre-marital counseling you were probably cautioned not to expect everything to be perfect. This is the beginning of your married life, and life in any stage always brings some challenges and adjustments.

Usually the groom takes financial responsibility and plans the trip. But, as with all aspects of the wedding, each couple decides how they want to approach this decision. Careful attention to details will cut down on unwanted surprises and frustrating situations. Planning should be divided into two parts: the first night and the honeymoon or trip itself.

THE FIRST NIGHT

Usually after all of the planning, the showers and groom honoring, the special times with the family, and the wedding and reception, a bride and groom are too exhausted to drive a long distance. You might want to plan to spend the first night somewhere close. If you are traveling by plane or train the next day, arrange a place close to the airport or depot. The groom should ask someone to pick up any clothes or items that you will not be taking on the rest of your honeymoon.

Since many hotels offer wedding-night packages, you should shop around. Envision your first night. Do you want to be in a luxury suite or in a place where you can take a walk? Decide on the type of place that will meet your needs. Be sure to ask at tuxedo rental shops if they have any special arrangements with hotels. Even though they don't advertise it, many shops are willing to negotiate if you are renting several tuxedos from them. For instance, you might ask for a complimentary night at a hotel instead of a free groom's tuxedo. Don't be afraid to negotiate. Most wedding places have more room for negotiation than they freely admit.

You may want to fulfill some specific dreams on your wedding night. For example, my husband always dreamed of carrying his bride over the hotel threshold in full wedding regalia. So that's what we did. Our arrival at the hotel in our wedding clothes inspired the management to upgrade our room!

Many hotels will place items in your room before you arrive. You could arrange for flowers, a bottle of champagne, a tape deck and meaningful tapes, or whatever you might like. The key to a successful first night is imaginative planning—and a patient attitude if it doesn't all work out the way you had planned.

THE HONEYMOON

Look in the travel sections of the local papers for airline specials. Check often because some specials only run for a day or two. If you are a careful shopper, you can really save a lot of money.

You might have a friend who owns a cottage in the mountains or at the beach. If he or she were willing to loan it to you, you could cut down on expenses and still have a special secluded time together. A word of caution: If you are using a privately owned cottage, make sure it is equipped for a comfortable honeymoon. An unheated cottage in the middle of winter could make for some tough times.

Check the Yellow Pages for vacation outlets or discount vacations. Also people sometimes sell tickets or vacation packages in the want ads. Be careful when buying these, though. Often, people will try to sell you tickets or vacations that cannot be resold. If in doubt, ask the seller for the name and address of the originator of the ticket or vacation package. Then you can call the place to find out if it is transferable. You would be a sad couple if you ended up standing on the dock waving to all of the happy travelers on a ship leaving for the Bahamas—without you.

If you are planning to leave the country, be sure to update your passports or visas in plenty of time. In this case, the bride can choose

51

to travel in her maiden name or bring along a copy of the marriage certificate. As laws do change, you should check with the passport office in advance. Also, it would be wise to educate yourself on customs, culture, travel tips and any sentences that may be important to translate like, "Where is the bathroom?" You can find information on different countries through the passport office or a travel agency. They can also tell you if you need any vaccinations before entering the country. NOTE: Count the emotional cost of traveling abroad. You will already be making a dramatic change in your life. An unfamiliar setting might not be the best for this special time of transition.

WHEREVER YOU GO, PLAN AHEAD

Think through details such as:

1. Housing
2. Transportation
3. Itinerary
4. Budget for daily spending
5. Traveler's checks
6. Letting your bride know how to dress (if your destination is a surprise)
7. Converter for plug-in appliances if you are traveling abroad (shavers, hair dryers, curling irons, irons, etc.)
8. Location of the American Embassy (just in case . . .)
9. Maps, language books for travelers
10. Transportation to and from the airport

Whatever route you decide to take, you would be wise to seek free advice from professionals in the travel industry. You could also get some helpful tips from couples who have recently returned from their honeymoon as well as older, more seasoned travelers. Take the time to research and plan. Then enjoy. BON VOYAGE!!

Chapter 9

BEING THOUGHTFUL AFTER THE WEDDING

Even though this chapter addresses things to be done after the wedding, it ought to be read long before the wedding. Begin early to prepare your heart for expressions of gratitude to family and friends once the wedding is over.

In your desire to make a dramatic storybook exit, don't forget to thank your family and bridesmaids. Many of them will have traveled long distances to be with you. It is, of course, your special day, but as a disciple, you should make sure others feel special too. Out-of-town people may not see you again for a while, and they will feel a sense of emptiness if you do not take a moment to tell them good-bye.

Another time to acknowledge them is during your honeymoon. Yes, your honeymoon! Although in many ways you may "only have eyes" for each other, you should remember that others are a big part of your life together. Take a few minutes to send a card or telegram to your family and to close friends expressing your love for each other and for them. Parents especially want to know that you arrived safely.

Now imagine that you have just come home from your honeymoon. Careful wedding budgeting and shopping for services is a mere memory. After an exciting and refreshing time away, you are ready to start your new life together in your own home. Be careful not to move so quickly out of the pre-wedding mode that you forget all of the people who served you in so many ways during the preparations. Hopefully you will have kept a list of the people who gave so generously to you. Remember your roommate who drove all over creation to find just the right ribbon to go in the flower girl's hair? How about your friends who ran all kinds of errands for you in that final week and then prepared a wonderful dinner on your return?

Use your list to help you send special thank-you notes. Take someone out to lunch as expression of your gratitude. Somehow let each person know that you appreciate his/her help. Do not take it for granted. These people have busy lives, but they joyfully sacrificed to help and honor you during this special time. It's not that they expect something in return. But they will certainly be encouraged as they see your thankful heart.

Now, again, imagine driving up to your new home or apartment. As you walk through the door, your eyes stop on the beautiful shower gifts that you received. Then you unpack your suitcase—most of the contents were also gifts. As you look with wondering eyes, you see a stack of unopened gifts that were brought to the wedding. And what about all of the cards that hold money gifts? God has richly blessed you in the start of your new marriage. The money will certainly help the state of your new empty joint bank account.

Imagination aside, plan for thank-you's now. Thank-you cards should be individually handwritten, expressing the true gratitude that you feel. This is a must. For the next two or three weeks, take your gift list with you wherever you go, along with a stack of cards and envelopes. Whenever you have an opportunity, write, write, write. It helps to start writing thank-you's as the gifts come and as people help you in your preparations. Add special touches to your thank-you notes—a snapshot of the happy couple, a handmade card, a simple red rose, etc. At any rate, as a disciple, do not neglect to express thankfulness. This is the very heart of our gracious, giving God.

After taking the time to express your heartfelt thanks to all those who have touched your life, you will then be ready to share your insight and experience with other engaged couples as you and your husband spend your lives together building new memories and enjoying new experiences.

The Author

Nancy Orr lives in Wilmington, Massachusetts, with her husband Jim and two daughters, Meghan and Tiffany. She was trained as a piano performer and has performed throughout the U.S., Canada, and Europe. She has been a wedding consultant since 1973 and has counseled several hundred couples regarding wedding plans.

HELPS

The Wedding Of

_____ - _____

Date, Time, Place: _____

Reception: _____

Coordinator: _____

EVENT COORDINATORS

Shower(s)/Groom Honoring   Rehearsal

_____   _____

_____   _____

Wedding Day   Reception

_____   _____

_____   _____

WEDDING PARTY

Groom_____   Bride_____

Best Man_____   Maid of Honor_____

Groomsmen_____   Matron of Honor_____

Groomsmen_____   Bridesmaids_____

_____   _____

_____   _____

_____   _____

_____   _____

_____   _____

Minister(s)_____

Flower girl_____   Ring bearer_____

VIP PHONE LIST

	Work	Home
Bride		
Groom		
Florist		
Cake baker		
Photographer		
Church Office		
Reception Office		
Rental Facility		
Coordinators		
Music Director		

Wedding Budget

REHEARSAL	Budget	Actual	FLOWERS	Budget	Actual
Facility fee			Bride's bouquet		
Musician(s)			Tossing bouquet		
Sound system			Cake-table flowers		
Parking			Reception centerpieces		
Servers			Pew decorations		
Food ($ x #) =			Altar		
Decorations			Corsages, moms. . .		
Clean-up			Boutonnieres		
Favors/gifts			Bridesmaids'		
subtotal			Rehearsal. . .		
CEREMONY			Flower girl basket		
Marriage license			subtotal		
Musician(s)					
Facility fee			PHOTOGRAPHY		
Custodian			Engagement portrait		
Minister's fee			Formal bridal portrait		
Candelabra			Wedding album		
Flowers			Wedding photographer		
Ring bearer's pillow			Proofs		
Blood test			Extra prints		
Dressing room food			Videographer		
subtotal			Extra video tapes		
			Cassette recording		
			subtotal		

59

RINGS	Budget	Actual	GROOM'S CLOTHES	Budget	Actual
Groom's			Formalwear		
Bride's			Shirt		
subtotal			Shoes		
			Accessories		
BRIDE'S CLOTHES			subtotal		
Trousseau					
Gown			RECEPTION		
Headpiece, veil			Facility site		
Shoes			Custodian		
Gloves			Sound system/music		
Lingerie, hosiery			Decorations		
Handbag			Napkins		
Jewelry			Tablecloths		
Garter			Plates		
			Cups (hot and cold)		
			Silverware		
subtotal			Toast		
			Ice		
BEAUTY			Food		
Manicure/pedicure			Servers		
Facial			Parking		
Hairstyling			Emcee		
Makeup			subtotal		
subtotal					

STATIONERY	Budget	Actual	MISC.	Budget	Actual
Invitations, enclosures					
Postage					
Thank-you notes					
Programs					
Personal stationery					
Announcements					
Personalized. . .etc.					
Souvenir cake boxes					
Maps (photocopying)					
subtotal					
			subtotal		
			TOTAL BUDGET		
			TOTAL ACTUAL		

Money-Saving Ideas

Order of Ceremony

Wedding Day Checklist

I. ORGANIZATION

A. Order of events (have it written down and given to key people)

B. Wedding party told to arrive two hours early

C. Bride's runner is _____

D. Program (optional, plan for two-thirds of those attending)

   1. handing it out is _____
   2. producer is _____, and cost is _____

E. Parking Usher is _____

   1. assistants are _____
   2. they should arrive 45 minutes before ceremony starts

F. Custodian/head cleaner is _____

   1. bring supplies as needed (garbage bags, cleaners, rags)
   2. make sure building is clean both before and after

G. Dressing-room food (protein snack)

H. Bride's assistant is ____   _____

I. Keeper of the rings is _____

J. Tuxedo return is responsibility of _____

II. PHYSICAL ENVIRONMENT/ACCESSORIES

A. Guest-book/Gift-table registrars are _____
   Responsible for book, pen, table, special touches and
   transportation of gifts to couple's home

B. Minister (fee paid when)

C. Photographer is _____

   1. fee paid when
   2. photos when
   3. videographer (optional) is _____

D. Musicians (fee paid when)

E. Sound technician is _____

F. Lighting (check out to match mood)

G. Florist is _____

   1. money needed _____
   2. delivery time is _____
   3. runner (optional) is _____

H. Get-away car/limo

   1. decorations (check with best man and/or family)
   2. special touches inside (check with groom)
   3. driver is _____

Reception Checklist

I. ORGANIZATION

A. Emcee is _____
   (possibly best man, minister, disc jockey or band leader)

B. Order of events (have it written down)

C. Exit trimmings

   1. birdseed (?)

   2. honeymoon luggage delivered by _____

   3. key to apartment left with _____

   4. return of get-away limo

   5. picking up couple upon return is _____

D. Cake (plan on cake for 1/2 to 2/3 of the people expected)

   1. baker is _____

   2. delivery time is _____

   3. deposit_____, balance _____

   4. make sure table is secure

   5. remember the knife

   6. returnable parts?

E. Gift-table/guest-book registrars are

_____

_____

1. book, tablecloth, pen, special touches, card basket
2. responsible for delivering gifts to couple's home

F. Cash/check deposit (optional) can be made by
_____ to couple's account after
opening cards and removing monetary gifts.

II. PHYSICAL ENVIRONMENT/MOOD

A. Lighting (check it out ahead of time)

B. Decorations (colors, type, tablecloths, plates, napkins, silverware, cups, centerpieces)

C. Musicians
1. sound system
2. payment

III. FOOD

A. Chef is _____ph#_____
Address_____

1. time to arrive with food_____
2. ice needed?
3. leftover food to _____

B. Menu is

To the Minister:

RUNNING A SMOOTH AND EFFICIENT REHEARSAL

The rehearsal is usually the first time that the bridal party is together with all the family members. The tone that you set in this time can have a great effect and impact on the flow of the rehearsal dinner and the wedding. A wedding rehearsal should be warm but efficient. One hour is sufficient time for a rehearsal that includes setting up the wedding party, two recessionals and one processional. But how can this be done?

1. Set a realistic time for the rehearsal to begin. When deciding the rehearsal time with the bride and groom, these things should be taken into consideration:

   a. What time can the church or hall accommodate you? Some places may have another rehearsal going on before or after yours, so the couple should consult the church.

   b. How many people in the wedding party are coming from a considerable distance from work or from out of town? If the location is not easily accessible by public transportation, is far away, or is in an obscure location, scheduling an early rehearsal won't ensure one. Because of later arrivals, in a situation like those mentioned above, you'll find yourselves waiting for stragglers. In this case, a 6:30 or 7:00 rehearsal would be wise.

2. Once all of the rehearsal guests are there, begin with a prayer. This immediately sets the tone and it pulls all of the people together. This is a great time to have the bride and groom introduce everyone and for you to ask for everyone's attention and cooperation. It is sometimes necessary to remind people that this night and the following day are a time to encourage the bride and groom and to put any other issues aside.

3. With the tone set, the next step is to set up the wedding party. For this, you will need:

   a. a roll of masking tape
   b. all of the women wearing their wedding shoes
   c. a basic idea of how to place the attendants (in couples, or men on one side and women on the other)—bride and groom's option
   d. a stand-in bride (optional)
   e. idea of how couple wishes to be placed (facing you or facing audience)

   You would be wise to discuss these things with the couple to find out their wishes. Every wedding is individual and there are many, many ways to vary it. Allow the couple the freedom to decide. To set up the wedding party, first line men up by height and women by height, with the exception of the maid or matron of honor and the best man. Then it is much easier to arrange them.

4. Once arranged, place a small piece of masking tape on the floor underneath one toe of each person.

5. At this time, decide who is pulling the runner, who is escorting the mothers out, and how to escort the women (arm folded, woman's hand tucked into elbow). You can also instruct the men on how they will be entering (from the side, down the aisle, escorting the bridesmaids).

6. Now you can practice the recessional. The pace is quick, happy and smooth. Be sure to practice bringing the mothers out every time you practice the recessional. They are as important a part to practice as the the bridesmaids' exit. If you don't practice this, it is very likely that they will be forgotten on the wedding day, and the wedding is not over until the groom's mother is escorted out.

The recessional order traditionally is:

Bride and groom
Flower girl and ring bearer
Maid of honor and best man
Bridesmaids and ushers
Bride's mother (and others)
Groom's mother (and others)
Women traditionally are on the men's right as they leave.

7. Next, you are ready to practice the processional, beginning with the seating of the mothers (bride's mother last). If they are not lighting mothers' candles, then the groom, best man and minister enter, followed by the ushers, unless the ushers are coming down the aisle or escorting the bridesmaids. The pace should be slow, though not stilted. Remind the women to walk slowly, smile, and to keep their knees loose and flexible while standing, to prevent fainting. Remember the runner and make whatever arrangements are necessary to have a happy flower girl and ring bearer.

8. With one final recessional, you are ready to go to the rehearsal dinner.

9. Briefly decide what time the wedding party should arrive, remind ushers that part of being a groom's attendant is to usher the women in, one by one.

It is not necessary to have music during the rehearsal. Most musicians won't attend the rehearsal without extra fees. However, it is sometimes helpful, so the couple may wish to bring a boom box and tape to give the bridal party an idea of the music that will be playing during their entrance and exit. This will help people walk in at a pace that fits well with the music.

Some extra notes: At least a month before the ceremony, discuss your attire with the bride and groom, (i.e., whether you will wear a dark suit or a tuxedo which they will provide. Of course, you will want dark shoes and socks, as well.)

Ask the other Christians in their ministry to encourage and support the couple during the engagement and to celebrate with them by attending their wedding.

There is no guarantee of perfection even in the most professionally rehearsed weddings. As a minister, you can help to keep the atmosphere joyous and relaxed by your demeanor and poise. If someone does faint, if a ring does not arrive, if the bride arrives two hours late, it is not a national disaster. When the bride and groom become husband and wife, all that people will be focusing on is celebration. So keep perspective through whatever.

With prayer, preparation and knowledge of the couple's wishes, you will have an awesome, smooth rehearsal and a great wedding the next day.

OTHER NOTES

OTHER NOTES

OTHER NOTES

OTHER NOTES

OTHER NOTES

OTHER NOTES

OTHER NOTES